Produced in Grenada
by
AllyDay Creative Projects

Created & Written by: Dayliah Henry-Banthorpe
Photography & Graphic Design by: Alleyne Gulston

Revised Edition: ©2006
Telephone: 1 (473) 420-2132
Email: review.allyday_work@yahoo.com

Printed and bound in the United Kingdom

# Acknowledgements

Mark Banthorpe
Gary Birkett
Spice Island Beach Resort Kitchen Team
Sir Royston Hopkin KCMG
Nerissa Hopkin

Thanks to Rolf Hoschtialek for introducing me to the fascinating world of marketing, advertising and killer deadlines!
Special thanks to Sandra Coombs-Patterson for her unstinting support, encouragement and belief in all of my endeavours.
Very special thanks to my 'partner in crime' Alleyne Gulston without whom this project would have remained a 'good idea'.

*Dayliah Henry-Banthorpe*

... British chef, Mark Banthorpe, ... the morning after the hurricane, he cooked a slap-up breakfast over a blazing fire on the beach.

... I like Mark's cooking best because it is the most Caribbean, offering a sophisticated take on traditional dishes...

**Maggie O'Sullivan,** Sunday Telegraph
April 2, 2006

# A well kept secret...

Whenever anyone asks Mark how he became a chef he always regales them with the words below. I have always thought what a typical good common sense reason, which is very much in line with his character. So without his knowledge we have chosen to let him introduce himself to you in his own words:

*'When my dad thought it was about time I should be thinking about making a living, he told me he knew exactly how someone could ensure that they would never be out of a job.*

*'Feed 'em, bury 'em or clothe 'em and you'll never be out of work'.*

By virtue of the pages to follow, we don't have to tell you which choice he made. According to the way he tells it, his career in the kitchen did not begin as one of those great epiphany's, rather it has been far more of an ongoing discovery, a relationship which is still growing even after a span of some twenty four years. Based on that alone, you have to come to the conclusion that it must be the 'real thing,'

Mark's relationship with Grenada, Isle of Spice, and its bounty of ingredients and flavours has been nurtured and encouraged by the strong and idealistic vision of one of Grenada's premier hoteliers, Sir Royston Hopkin KCMG. His insistence on his establishment making full use of local flavours and produce and serving these at international dining standards has continually challenged and pushed the benchmark for both Mark and his team.

The recipes to follow show just how successfully this can be done in both simple and more complex terms to give the housewife, the cook and the connoisseur.....

## Tastes of Spice

9th November, 2006

Dear Mark

I wanted to be able to give you something you always say you will never have for this the event of our second wedding anniversary; your very own cookery book.

It's my way of thanking you for all the things I thought I would never have and now do through you: a fair and faithful friend, an understanding listener, a mentor and advisor, a very talented chef and most of all a husband whom I love dearly.

I hope that you will forgive some of the subterfuge it took to create this 'gift' for you. Be assured that no shortcuts were taken in researching and rechecking all those great recipes which you and your team have worked so hard to create and perfect. This was vital if we were to reproduce your passion for taste faithfully, even if we don't all have quite your presentational flair!

I hope you enjoy seeing your 'creations' on the printed page as much as we have enjoyed working to put them there. However, we fully expect that they will be leaping off the page and into the pots, pan, dishes and palates for which they were conceived, to be served in many kitchens other than your own.

A Very Happy Anniversary,


All my love, your wife

# Contents

# Plantain cornmeal
## and chilli fritters with a sour cream and lime dip

A big favourite in the Caribbean region, the jury is still out as to whether plantain, quite obviously part of the banana family, is a fruit or a vegetable. When choosing them, go for the ones which look black and bruised and you will usually find that these are the sweetest.

*"This highly nutritious fruit, or vegetable, contains calcium and potassium as well as vitamins A and C. With this being so healthy, better balance it out with a nice cold beer or glass of wine".*

### Choux Pastry
**Ingredients**
Serves 6

100ml milk
100ml water
80g butter
120g flour
3 eggs
pinch of salt & pinch of sugar

### Fritters
**Ingredients**

3 ripe plantain - medium size
114g cornmeal
½tsp hot dried chilli flakes
1tsp shado-beni
1½tsp hot pepper sauce
salt & pepper to taste

### Sour Cream and Lime Dip
**Ingredients**

100ml sour cream
2 limes - juice & grated zest
¼ tsp honey
salt & pepper to taste

Mix water, milk butter, salt & sugar in pan and bring to boil.
When boiling, add flour and mix vigorously until mix leaves the sides of the pan.
Beat for a further minute.
Remove from heat and leave to cool for one hour.
When cooled, beat in whole eggs one at a time and refrigerate until ready to use.

Peel and boil plantain until soft enough to pierce with a fork.
Mash the plantain and add to 200g of choux pastry mix along with cornmeal, chilli flakes, shado-beni & hot pepper sauce.
Season to taste.
Refrigerate until ready for use.
Take mix and roll into medium size balls.
Deep fry for 3 – 4 mins. until golden brown.

Add lime juice & zest slowly to sour cream, then add chives and honey.
Mix or blend thoroughly.
Add salt and pepper to taste.

# Twice baked callaloo
## souffle

### Base Mix
**Ingredients**
Serves 7

60g plain flour
60g butter
250ml (½ pint) milk
pinch ground cloves
1 bay leaf
(makes approx. 350g)

### Stewed Callaloo
**Ingredients**

400g callaloo*
2 onions - peeled & finely chopped
4 cloves of garlic - peeled & finely chopped
½ tin coconut milk (200ml)
8 seasoning peppers* - de-seeded & chopped
pinch of cinnamon
pinch of curry powder
1tsp thyme
1tbsp chives* - chopped
salt & pepper to taste

### Soufflé Finish
**Ingredients**

350g stewed callaloo
350g base mix
3 egg yolks
7 egg whites
100g melted butter & 100g breadcrumbs - to line soufflé moulds

*see glossary*

Melt butter and add flour to form a roux, leave to cool.
Boil milk with clove, bay leaf and pinch of salt.
Return roux to the heat and gradually add milk to form a thick paste.
Cook to disintegrate flour for 3 - 4 minutes and leave to cool.

Wash and clean callaloo. Sauté herbs, onions, garlic, peppers & chives in a tbsp of oil, until tender.
Add callaloo, coconut milk and spices.
Simmer over a low heat until soft and then add salt and pepper to taste.

Pre-heat oven to 150°C and prepare 1 bain-marie.
Line demi tasse (coffee cup) moulds with butter and put into fridge to set.
When set, brush with melted butter and line with breadcrumbs.
Mix the stewed callaloo and base mix together, add the egg yolks and mix thoroughly.
Whisk your egg whites with a pinch of salt until stiff and approximately double in volume.

Beat ⅓ of egg whites into callaloo mix to loosen mixture and then fold in remaining whites.
Drop into prepared moulds and smooth over tops.
Place moulds in bain-marie and cook at 150° - 160°C for approx. 35 - 45 minutes until risen and set.
Remove from the oven and leave to stand for approx 15 – 20 minutes.

Carefully remove the soufflés from the moulds.
To re-heat, place in a hot oven for 5 - 10 minutes and serve immediately.

# Devilled lambie

Yes it's true! This comes from the inside of those beautiful pink shells which are sold on the beaches. Don't worry. By the time you buy it, this member of the mollusk family, also known as conch, will probably be neatly packaged and ready for your cooking endeavours.

*"Its faintly sweet taste, meaty texture and ability to adopt the flavours it is seasoned with, make this a favourite island delicacy."*

## Lambie
### Ingredients
Serves 10

2 lambie - cleaned & tenderised
2tbsp seasoning mix (see pg 16)
2 onions – peeled & diced
1tbsp lime juice
salt & pepper to taste

## Sauce
### Ingredients

lambie stock
cornstarch
453g (1lb) cheddar cheese - grated
6 tomatoes – chopped
2tbsp parsley - chopped
2tbsp basil - chopped
2tbsp hot pepper sauce
2tbsp chives* - chopped

### Topping
284g breadcrumbs
70g grated parmesan cheese
50g butter - melted

Place lambie and all other ingredients in a pot and cover with water.
Cook until tender.
Remove from heat and chop roughly in a blender.
Strain cooking juices through a fine sieve and retain.

Boil stock and reduce by half.
Use cornstarch to thicken to the consistency of a thick gel.
Add remaining ingredients and season with salt and pepper.
Add the cooked lambie to the sauce and leave to cool.

Place lambie mix in a dish and heat through in microwave.
To make topping, rub all ingredients together until resembling a crumble/breadcrumb mix.
Top the lambie with bread crumb mix and bake in a hot oven until golden brown.

*see glossary*

8

# Deep fried tempura of marlin
## with pickled ginger & vegetable laces

Grenada has year round Marlin fishing and its very own Spice Island Billfish Tournament in January of each year. At this event, most of the fish caught are weighed and returned to their ocean home.

*"This firm fleshed fish is ideal for the recipe below or can be substituted with tuna or swordfish, all of which are readily available in Grenada and oftentimes straight from the boats of the local fishermen."*

### *Vegetable Laces*
**Ingredients**
Serves 4

8 x 30g of marlin - thinly cut
2tbsp seasoning mix (see pg 16)
50g each vegetable laces
(christophene, pumpkin, sweet potato,
green papaya & spring onions)
14g pickled ginger

### *Vegetable Marinade*
**Ingredients**
100ml white wine vinegar
150g white sugar
1tsp fish sauce
2 cloves garlic - finely chopped
2tsp sesame oil
100ml water
1tsp dried hot chilli flakes
2tsp fresh ginger - finely grated

### *Tempura Batter*
**Ingredients**

1 egg white
200ml soda water
150g rice flour
65g coconut - grated

Season marlin using seasoning mix and put to one side for at least 1 hour.

Peel each vegetable.
Next use a peeler to make the laces using long downwards strokes to create them

Combine all ingredients for vegetable marinade and bring to the boil. Use salt & five spice seasoning to taste. Simmer for 2 - 3 minutes.
Pour over vegetable laces and leave to marinate for 30 minutes.

Combine all batter ingredients as for a pancake mix.

Place fish in flour and cover.
Dust off flour and dip in batter shaking off any excess.
Deep fry fish for 2 – 3 minutes. Drain off any extra oil.

Place a portion of the vegetable laces in the centre of the plate.
Place fish on top and crown with pickled ginger.
Dress with remaining marinade from vegetable laces.

# Seafood broth
## with herb dumplings

Each island has its own variation of fish broth more commonly known as 'fish waters'. This of course is understandable as Grenada, 21 miles long by 12 miles wide, is surrounded by both the Caribbean Sea and Atlantic Ocean.

It is also common knowledge that the best fish for making 'waters' are the many varieties of 'red fish' like Rock Hind or Red Snapper. However, some of the smaller and more bony varieties are not fished commercially and so may be hard to find, unless you are fortunate enough to see the fishermen come in with their fresh catches along the Carenage, or at the fish market in St George's, Grenada's capital.

### Seafood Broth
**Ingredients**
Serves 6

473ml (1pint) of good fish stock
454g (1lb) of mixed seafood (shrimps, swordfish, lobster, tuna & mahi mahi)
1 cup of white wine
small cup of each diced vegetable (carrot, squash, christophene, sweet potato, okra & green beans)
3 large onions - finely diced
3 cloves of garlic – crushed
8 seasoning peppers* - chopped & de-seeded
1tsp each of chopped herbs (dill, parsley, shado beni*)
75g chives* - chopped
1 lemon - juice only
salt & pepper to taste

### Herb Dumplings
**Ingredients**

454g flour
1 cup of water
2tbsp each herb (shado beni*, basil, thyme, parsley)

**F**ry onions in a touch of olive oil.
Add garlic, seasoning peppers.
Cook without colour and add diced vegetables, **except** the okra and green beans.
Add white wine, turn up heat and reduce wine by half.
Add fish stock, bring to boil and then allow to simmer
Add mixed seafood and poach for 2 minutes.
Add juice of lemon, fresh herbs and chives.
Season to taste.

**T**ake flour, add herbs & seasonings and make a well in the centre.
Pour water in slowly and mix to form dough.
Knead for 3 – 4 minutes.
Roll into small balls and cook in broth 5 minutes before serving.
NB. Add the okra and green beans now, along with the dumplings, as these become tender very quickly.

*see glossary

# Cream of Christophene
## soup

Christophene is simply a sub-tropical member of the squash family and is normally used here in Grenada as a vegetable, as in this recipe. However, although many of us here in the Caribbean use christophene as a vegetable, it is actually a fruit which resembles an oversized grooved pear and can be used in exactly the same way.

*"Here's a challenge for you, take your favourite apple pie or apple crumble recipe and substitute the apple with christophene. You'll be amazed at the results and it's guaranteed your guests will be hard pressed to tell the difference."*

### Cream of Christophene Soup
**Ingredients**
Serves 8 - 10

6 christophene - peeled, cored & chopped
2tbsp seasoning mix (see pg 16)
3 large onions chopped
946ml (2 pints) vegetable stock
236ml (½ pint) of cream
120g butter
salt & pepper to taste

Sweat christophene with butter, seasoning mix and onion for 5 – 10 minutes on low heat.
Add stock and bring to boil.
Simmer for 25 minutes.
Add cream, liquidise and season to taste.
Serve hot.

### Basic Seasoning Mix
**Ingredients**

4 cloves of garlic
29g of ginger
½ onion – peeled & chopped
small bunch of ground basil
6 seasoning peppers*
1 litre vegetable oil
2tbsp vinegar
salt & pepper

Blend all ingredients together and use as required.

*see glossary

# Butternut squash
## soup with roasted garlic

This member of the squash family is interchangeable with calabaza which is a pumpkin-like vegetable grown in the Caribbean and Central and South America. Its firm succulent flesh is bright orange and has a somewhat sweet flavour.

Butternut squash or members of its family are readily available in markets and supermarkets around the island.

### *Butternut Squash Soup with Roasted Garlic*
**Ingredients**
Serves 6

1 squash – approx 908g (2lb) - de-seeded & chopped
3 onions – chopped
4 cloves of garlic - crushed
1 leek – shredded
1.4 litres (3pints) vegetable stock
200ml cream
120g butter
6 seasoning peppers* de-seeded & chopped
1tsp each cumin seeds, coriander seeds & fresh ginger - peeled and grated
salt & pepper to taste

Melt butter, add vegetables and all seasonings and sweat for 10 – 15 minutes.
Add stock and bring to boil, then simmer on low heat for 20 - 30 minutes.
Once all vegetables are tender, place in liquidiser.
Blend until smooth.
Add cream and season to taste.

### *Roasted garlic*
**Ingredients**

Garlic cloves (how many depends on how friendly you are or wish to remain!)

Slice garlic finely.
Place on greaseproof paper and put in oven.
Roast for 10 – 15 minutes or until just brown.
Sprinkle over soup and serve immediately.

*see glossary*

18

# Coconut and pineapple
## bisque

Cold soups do not always come so easily to the Caribbean palate, but here is a lovely blend of two ingredients often viewed as synonomous with this part of the world.

To select a ripe pineapple, look for a soft orange complexion. Pull on the top leaves, they should come off easily with a tug. Smell the bottom of the fruit and its sweet fragrance should be easily detectable. Marry this with the coconut, one of the most popular fruits found in the Caribbean which grows throughout the year on tall palm trees. You have a sure winner.

*"By edict of the Grenada government, buildings can rise no higher than a coconut palm - which is even more reason for this being one of our favourite fruits as its palms beautify our beaches and countryside."*

### *Coconut and Pineapple Bisque*
**Ingredients**
Serves 8 - 10

1 tin coconut milk (414ml)
1 tin crushed pineapple in own juice
½tbsp limejuice
118ml (¼ pint) sour cream
1 fresh pineapple – finely chopped and macerated with dark rum, syrup and lime.
1 dry coconut – peeled and finely grated, mix with macerated pineapple.

Blend first 4 ingredients together – chill overnight.
Use one inch pipe/mould and press macerated pineapple mixture into this, place in soup bowl and remove mould.
Pour blended ingredients around mixture and serve.

# Pigeon pea and sweet potato salad
## with shado beni and honey mustard dressing

Pigeon peas are widely cultivated in many tropical and sub-tropical regions of the world. In Grenada the plants start to flower around October and the peas are usually harvested from January through to March/April. If any arrive earlier they are greatly sought after, especially for use during the December holiday season. Most often the peas may be found in their dried form, but they are also delicious fresh.

*"As a matter of interest, pigeon peas have a reputation for being slightly narcotic, possibly accounting for very deep naps after lunch... a favourite Sunday afternoon pastime of many here in the Isle of Spice."*

### Pigeon Pea and Sweet Potato Salad
**Ingredients**
Serves 6

2 sweet potatoes
200g pigeon peas
2 medium onions - chopped
3 cloves of garlic - crushed
1 bayleaf
1 sprig of thyme
salt & pepper to taste

**Peel** and cube sweet potato.
Boil until tender with a bite!
Place pigeon peas in a pan of water, add onions, garlic, bayleaf and thyme and bring to the boil.
Turn down to a simmer and cook until tender.
When peas are cooked, drain and mix with sweet potato.
Add dressing to mix, season to taste and refrigerate until ready for use.
Serve this chilled.

### Shado Beni and Honey Mustard Dressing
**Ingredients**

100ml olive oil
30ml white wine vinegar.
2tbsp Dijon mustard
2tbsp honey
2tsp shado beni*
4 seasoning peppers* - chopped
1tsp each - parsley, basil, celery tops - chopped

*see glossary*

**Whisk** mustard and slowly add in the oil.
Whilst continuing to whisk, add all remaining ingredients.
Season with salt and pepper to taste.

# Marinated green papaya salad
## with guava vinaigrette

A piece of ripe papaya is one of the most popular and healthy breakfast dishes in the Caribbean, Grenada no exception. In addition to this, there are various medicinal uses for papaya including treatments for maladies ranging from rheumatism to warts!

Mature green papaya contains more vitamin A than carrots, more vitamin C than oranges and has abundant vitamin B and E factors. Also used as a meat tenderiser, this fruit is extremely versatile.

### *Marinated Green Papaya Salad with Guava Vinaigrette*
**Ingredients**
Serves 4 - 6

1 large green papaya (2lbs)
100g chives* - chopped finely
3 cloves of garlic
½ stick of lemon grass - chopped finely
1 stick ginger - peeled & crushed
2tbsp shado beni* - chopped
4 limes -juice & zest
1tsp hot pepper sauce

### Guava Vinaigrette
65ml guava pulp
2tsp Dijon mustard
2tbsp sherry vinegar
115ml (¼ pint) olive oil
salt & pepper to taste

Peel and cut papaya into thin strips.
Blanch the strips in a large pan of boiling salted water for 20 - 30 seconds.
Refresh in cold water and drain.
Add all remaining ingredients including lime juice and grated zest.
Marinate for 1 – 2 hours.

Blend the mustard, sherry vinegar and olive oil using a stick blender or liquidizer.
Add this mixture gradually to the guava pulp so that all the ingredients blend to a smooth consistency.
Use salt and pepper to taste.

*see glossary

26

# Orange and grapefruit salad
## with sweet basil dressing

### *Orange and Grapefruit*
**Ingredients**
Serves 6

4 oranges
4 grapefruit

### *Sweet Basil Dressing*
**Ingredients**

118ml (¼ pint) of water
85g sugar
2tbsp honey
5 large basil leaves – finely shredded

Peel and segment all of the fruit.

Place water, sugar and honey in pan to boil for 5 minutes until a light syrup consistency is reached.
Cool syrup. Whilst still warm add basil as this will aid in quicker infusion.
*(Don't add basil whilst the syrup is hot as this will cause the basil to turn black.)*
Arrange fruit on plate and drizzle each with a liittle syrup.

# Pan Fried Breast of Chicken

## Stuffed with a Shrimp and Cashew Nut Mousse

### Pan Fried Breast of Chicken Stuffed with a Shrimp and Cashew Nut Mousse
**Ingredients**
Serves 4

4 chicken breasts - skinned & trimmed
1 egg white
100g white chicken meat
60g raw shrimp - peeled & chopped
40g cashew nuts - toasted & chopped
100ml double cream
20g tomato concasse
2tbsp seasoning (see pg 16)
juice of ½ lemon
100g butter

### Sauce
**Ingredients**

40g butter
1 onion - finley chopped
½ cup dry vermouth
2tbsp seasoning mix
1tsp tomato paste
450ml fish fumet* (stock)
1tsp hot pepper sauce
220ml double cream
10 basil leaves - shredded
1tsp shado-beni* - finely chopped

Use the 100g of white chicken meat, egg white and cream to make a light farce/mince.

Fold in the chopped shrimp, cashew nuts and tomato concasse* and season to taste.

Remove the fillets from the chicken breasts and flatten between 2 pieces of cling film using the flat blade of a heavy knife.

Open up the chicken breasts and stuff with the farce.

Replace the fillets, shape, season & chill.

Stew the stuffed chicken in butter and lemon juice – keeping it very light in colour.

Place on your plates and dress with sauce.

Try serving this dish with fine green beans, steamed until tender and tossed in butter or olive oil along with fried coo-coo (polenta)

Melt the butter, add the onion and seasoning mix, cook without colour until tender.

Add tomato paste and then the vermouth.

Reduce this sauce by two thirds.

Add fish fumet, return to the boil and reduce once again by two thirds.

Add the cream and bring to the boil. Reduce until the sauce reaches the consistency of cold oil.

Strain sauce by passing it through a fine sieve.

Add shredded basil leaves and season to taste.

Cover with buttered grease proof paper and warm gently when ready for use.

*see glossary

# Oil Down

*"This 'one pot' meal is Grenada's national dish and culinary gift to the world – whatever variations other islands may have, the true home of this dish is the Isle of Spice. Not only that, but every Grenadian home has its own touch of 'je ne sais quoi' which makes their version the very best!"*

### Oil Down
**Ingredients**
Serves 6 - 8

1kg chicken – preferably back and neck
100g salt beef - soaked in water overnight & par-boiled
100g pig tail - soaked in water overnight & par-boiled
200g breadfruit - pared & cut into large pieces
200g green bananas - peeled
50g salt fish - cooked & flaked
25g seasoning peppers* - chopped
25g garlic - peeled & chopped
1 sprig of thyme
25g chives* - chopped
50g callaloo
50g carrot - chopped
50g okra - chopped
2 tins coconut milk (414ml each)
½tbsp saffron
10 large dumplings - made by mixing flour & water.

Season chicken and lay in pot. (*See pg 16 for seasoning mix*)
Wash salted meat, cut into pieces and lay in pot.
Cover meat with a layer of breadfruit, green banana and carrots and seasonings. (NB Rub a small amount of oil into your hands before peeling the breadfruit and green bananas.)
Continue placing alternate layers of meat, salt fish, breadfruit, green banana, okra and carrots mixed with seasonings. Place your dumplings on the top.
Mix coconut milk, curry and saffron and pour entire mixture over all the ingredients layered in the pot.
Cook on a medium to low heat for approximately 2 hours. Simmer until most of the liquid has been absorbed. Spread callaloo over the top of all the ingredients and cover tightly with a fitted lid.
Simmer on low heat for approximately 1 - 1½ hours or until all liquid has been absorbed.

NB. You can make your own coconut milk by mixing water with the grated white meat inside of dry coconuts and then pouring this mixture though a sieve, utilising the liquid only.

*see glossary

# Lobster tail
## with mango and tamarind sauce

### Lobster
**Ingredients**
Serves 4

Two x 1kg lobsters
50g ginger – chopped
50g garlic – crushed
4 thyme sprigs
50g basil
10 seasoning peppers* - de-seeded & chopped
2 bunches of scallions*
50ml olive oil
salt & pepper to taste

### Mango and Tamarind Sauce
**Ingredients**

25ml olive oil
50g butter
lobster heads
1tsp tamarind paste
2 cloves garlic
100g ginger
1 onion - finely chopped
200ml fish stock
1 lime - juice & grated zest
2 fresh ripe mangoes
200ml heavy cream
200ml dry vermouth

*see glossary*

**I**f using live lobster, you may wish to place them in the freezer for a couple of hours as this is a more humane way of killing them than in boiling water.
Remove the tails by twisting and pulling off.
With a heavy knife, cut across through the tail into 2 inch sections.
Blend all the remaining ingredients.
Marinate the lobster tails in the blended ingredients for 2 - 3 hours.
Split the lobster heads in two and remove the filters and intestines.
Crush the shell finely and reserve for use in the sauce.

**F**ry the crushed lobster shell in butter & oil for 3 - 4 minutes.
Add ginger and garlic and cover pan on low heat for 5 - 10 minutes. Shake occasionally to stop ingredients from sticking.
Remove lid and add vermouth. Reduce by two thirds and add fish stock.
Reduce again by two thirds and add tamarind paste, lime juice & zest, mangoes and cream.
Bring to the boil, simmer for 10 minutes and then leave to stand for 20 minutes.
Sieve sauce through a fine strainer.
Season with salt & pepper to taste.

**P**an fry lobsters in a little olive oil and butter until they begin to change colour. Place in oven and cook for 7 - 8 minutes. When cooked, loosen the inside of the shell around the meat.
Dress the meat and plate with sauce.
You may wish to sprinkle some finely chopped herbs and serve with breadfruit mash & steamed asparagus.

# Roast saddle of rabbit

## filled with chicken mousse, with ravioli of leg, callaloo & garlic

### Roast Saddle of Rabbit filled with Chicken Mousse
**Ingredients**
Serves 4

1 Rabbit (remove legs and saddle
– ask butcher)
453g (1lb) of callaloo
1 chicken breast
1 egg
473ml (1pint) full cream
4 cloves of garlic
½tsp saffron
salt & pepper to taste

### Ravioli Paste
**Ingredients**

125g bread flour (strong white flour)
125g cornmeal
4 egg yolks
2 whole eggs
2tsp salt

### Ravioli Filling
**Ingredients**

rabbit legs
1 onion – chopped
1 carrot – chopped
1 stick of celery – chopped
237ml (½ pint) of red wine
946ml (2 pints) chicken stock
350g stewed callaloo (see pg 6)

Place all ravioli paste ingredients in a food processor and blend until the mix resembles small breadcrumbs.
Remove from machine and knead to form dough.
Continue to knead for 5 more minutes.
Wrap dough tightly in cling film.
Refrigerate for a minimum of one hour prior to use.

Take the rabbit legs, place in a large cooking pot and brown using butter.
Add onion, carrot and celery.
Continue to brown for a further 10 minutes, add red wine and chicken stock.
Cover and place in moderate oven for 2 hours.

Take cooked rabbit legs and remove flesh from the bones – this should fall off easily.
Flake meat and mix with a touch of chicken stock and 125g of stewed callaloo.
Season to taste with salt and pepper and refrigerate.

## Ravioli

Roll out ravioli paste thinly with a pasta machine and place on a floured board.

Cut 8 circles of pasta with a metal cutter approx. 10cm in diameter.

Cut another 8 circles of pasta with a metal cutter approx. 6cm in diameter.

Place a tablespoon of the rabbit mix in the centre of the large pasta circle. Place the small pasta circle over the rabbit mix, brush the edges of the large circle with egg wash and bring the edges to meet the smaller circle.

Pinch the edges together and place on a floured tray until ready for use.

The ravioli should resemble a small pie shape, similar to a pork pie.

It can be cooked in advance in lots of boiling salted water. If you are doing so, refresh it in ice water. When cooked, place on a clean tray and chill until ready for use. It can be easily re-heated in a microwave.

## Saddle of Rabbit filled with Chicken Mousse

Take chicken breast and place in food processor with a pinch of salt.

Add egg and liquidize, gradually add cream.

Remove mixture from liquidizer and place in a metal bowl.

Add pepper and saffron and refrigerate until ready for use.

Take saddle and make an incision on the side, wiggle your knife in the incision to form a small pocket.

Season inside of pocket with salt and pepper. Use a piping bag to pipe in chicken and saffron mousse. Close pocket over to conceal mousse and then wrap in cling film. Roll and tie tightly as for a sausage. Refrigerate for a minimum of 30 minutes.

To cook, place rabbit sausage in a pan of cold water. Place on stove and bring to boil. When boiled, remove from heat and place in fridge to cool completely in the hot water. This will give you a perfectly cooked sausage.

**Stewed Callaloo**

**Garnish**

**Assembling the dish**

Stewed Callaloo
*(See page 6 for method) Use remainder of this from the ravioli filling as an accompaniment for this dish.*

**8** Cherry tomatoes, roasted.
Selection of roasted vegetables (christophene, sweet potato, breadfruit, carrots)

Place the sausage in a moderate oven for 15 minutes.
Roast your selected vegetables at the same time.
Strain juices left from the cooking of the rabbit legs and reduce by one third.
Place ravioli in a pan of boiling water for 3 – 4 minutes, then drain.
Place ravioli on a bed of stewed callaloo.
Remove rabbit sausage from oven and carve into two pieces, place on top of ravioli.
Garnish dish with roasted vegetable and cherry tomatoes.
Finish with rabbit jus over sausage and ravioli.

# Grilled shrimp
## with sweet corn puree and cajun salsa

### *Grilled Shrimp*
**Ingredients**
Serves 4

24 shrimp (16 - 20 per 1lb) peeled and de-veined
1cup seasoning (see pg 16)
1tsp dried chilli flakes
2tbsp lime juice
4 turns freshly ground black pepper

### *Sweetcorn Puree*
**Ingredients**

4 corn on the cob – boiled
4 onions – finely chopped
8tbsp extra virgin olive oil
3tbsp chopped chives*
3tsp chopped basil

### *Cajun Salsa*
**Ingredients**

1 cucumber– peeled, seeded & finely chopped
1 large red onion – finely chopped
4 tomatoes – seeded & diced
14g sun-dried tomatoes – chopped
1 each red, yellow & green bell pepper – finely chopped
2tbsp of honey
1tbsp each parsley & chives* – finely chopped
3tbsp extra virgin olive oil
2tbsp each - vegetable oil, cider vinegar, balsamic vinegar
4 garlic cloves – peeled & grated
1tbsp hot pepper sauce

**M**ix all ingredients together and leave to marinate over night.
Grill shrimp for 2 – 3 minutes.
These should be placed on top of sweetcorn purée. .

**B**oil corn and cut off niblets.
Place all ingredients in blender and bring to purée consistency.
You can place purée mix into small moulds or shape into rounds for presentation purposes if you wish.

**M**ix all ingredients together and allow to stand for 1 hour.
Use as required to dress shrimp and sweet corn purée.

**F**lavoured oils such as herb oil, red pepper oil and black wine or a sorrel reduction can be used for decoration/presentation purposes.

You can be as imaginative as you wish!

**I**n the adjacent photograph herb oil, popcorn and reduced balsamic vinegar have been used to decorate the dish.

*see glossary*

# Rack of lamb on a mash of sweet potato

## scented with garlic and rosemary

*Rack of Lamb on a Mash of Sweet Potato Scented with Garlic and Rosemary*
**Ingredients**
Serves 4

1 best end of lamb - French trimmed*
4 cloves of garlic
4 sprigs of rosemary

2 large sweet potatoes
50g butter

4 pieces of buttenut squash
75g butter
pinch of ground cinnamon
1tsp brown sugar

1 ripe plantain
vegetable oil for frying

**For sauce**

lamb trimmings & bones
150g mire poix*
3 cloves garlic
2 sprigs thyme
50g butter
½ tsp tomato paste
½ tsp redcurrant jelly
100ml red wine
473ml (1 pint) lamb stock
2tsp arrowroot

Brown the lamb in hot fat and then place in a pan with the bones facing down.
Add garlic and rosemary to the pan and cook in oven at 370°F until pink. Approx. 10 -15 minutes
Remove from oven and leave to rest.

Peel and cut sweet potato into even size pieces.
Cover with cold water add salt and bring to the boil.
When tender, drain and mash with butter.

Melt the butter and toss squash, cinnamon and sugar.
Place squash on a baking tray and bake at 360°F until golden in colour and tender.

Peel ripe plantain, slice and fry.

Fry the mire poix, lamb trimmings & bones and garlic in butter, until just beginning to brown.
Add tomato paste, red currant jelly and red wine.
Reduce to a syrup consistency.
Add lamb stock and thyme and reduce by two thirds.
Pass through a fine strainer.
Mix arrowroot with a liitle water and use to thicken sauce until it reaches the consistency of cold oil.
Season to taste.

Arrange the squash, sweet potato mash and plantain on a plate.
Cut the lamb into four portions and arrange on plates.
Dress the lamb with sauce as required.

*see glossary*

44

# Grilled swordfish with a soft herb crust
## accompanied by pumpkin ravioli with lime butter

Swordfish, when cooked properly, is a beautiful fish to eat. In the Mediterranean you would use olive oil, garlic and tomatoes and not fuss with it too much. In this recipe we use a soft herb crust over the fish and cook it in a hot oven for 3 - 5 minutes. The crust adds flavour and texture to the finished dish and the ravioli brings a dash of added elegance to it.

### Sword Fish
**Ingredients**
Serves 6

6 x 140g pieces of swordfish
100g seasoning (see pg 16)

*T*rim swordfish to equal sized pieces and mix in seasoning, place in fridge and leave for at least 2 hours before cooking.

### Herb Crust
**Ingredients**

125g breadcrumbs
25g parsley
25g chives*
15g coriander*
2 cloves of garlic – finely grated
40g unsalted butter
freshly ground black pepper to taste
1 lime – grated zest only
1 egg yolk

*P*lace breadcrumbs, herbs, garlic, salt, pepper and lime zest in a food processor and blend until it reaches a fine breadcrumb consistency.
Add melted butter and egg yolks and blend briefly until mix binds.
Cover the back of a flat baking pan with a double layer of cling film.
Place the mix on the cling-filmed tray and flatten slightly with your hand.
Cover flattened mix with another double sheet of cling-film and using a rolling pin, roll until approximately 4.5mm thick.

*see glossary

## Herb Crust
**Continued**

Place in the freezer for two hours.
Remove mix from the freezer and cut into portions equivalent to fish portions.
Place herb crust on top of fish.
Arrange on greased tray and bake in hot oven – 200°C for 4 – 6 minutes.
Serve immediately.

## Ravioli Paste
**Ingredients**

125g bread flour (strong white flour)
125g cornmeal
4 egg yolks
2 whole eggs
2 tsp salt

Place all ingredients in a food processor and blend until the mix resembles small breadcrumbs.
Remove from machine and knead to form dough.
If the mix feels too dry add a little water, you should have a smooth non-sticky dough.
Continue to knead for 5 more minutes.
Wrap dough tightly in cling film.
Refrigerate for a minimum of one hour prior to use.

## Ravioli Filling
**Ingredients**

250g pumpkin
1 bunch chives* finely chopped
2 cloves garlic – finely grated
15ml olive oil
pinch of ground cinnamon
pinch of ground cloves
50g grated parmesan
1tsp chopped coriander*

Peel and dice pumpkin into 1 inch squares, mix with a little melted butter, salt and freshly ground pepper.
Sprinkle with the spices and roast in a medium oven until tender.
Heat the oil and cook the chives and garlic, without browning.
Place the pumpkin in a bowl with cooked chives and onion mix, along with parmesan.
Break ingredients with fork but not to smooth consistency.
The mixture should be fairly dry, not too moist.

## Ravioli Method

Roll out ravioli paste thinly with a pasta machine and place on a floured board.

Cut 8 circles of pasta with a metal cutter approx. 10cm in diameter.

Cut another 8 circles of pasta with a metal cutter approx. 6cm in diameter.

Place a tablespoon of the pumpkin mix in the centre of the large pasta circle. Place the small pasta circle over the pumpkin mix.

Brush the edges of the large circle with egg wash and bring the edges to meet the smaller circle.

Pinch the edges together and place on a floured tray until ready for use.

The ravioli should resemble a small pie shape, similar to a pork pie.

It can be cooked in advance in lots of boiling salted water. If you are doing so refresh it in ice water when cooked.

Place on a clean tray and chill until ready for use. It can be easily re-heated in a microwave.

## Lime Butter Sauce
### Ingredients

200ml fish stock
100ml white wine
100g unsalted butter
100g finely chopped onion
2 sprigs fresh thyme
2 limes - grated zest & juice
1 tbsp. chopped chives*
1 tsp butter

Use the tsp butter to cook the onion without browning.

Add the wine, fish stock and thyme and bring mixture to the boil.

Add the lime zest and juice and reduce the mix until it reaches syrup consistency.

Start whisking in the butter in small amounts away from the heat until the total amount is used.

Season the sauce to taste with salt, ground white pepper and a pinch of cayenne pepper.

Finish the sauce with the chopped chives and reserve for use.

Take care not to boil the sauce or it will separate.

*see glossary

48

# Roasted Duck Breast
## with Pigeon Peas and Beetroot Confit

### Roasted Duck Breast with Pigeon Peas and Beetroot Confit
**Ingredients**
Serves 4

4 trimmed duck breasts
2tbsp seasoning (see pg 16)

150g pigeon peas (see pg 24)
60g pancetta - diced
1tbsp parsley - chopped
50ml port wine
75ml chicken stock

300ml orange juice
150g cooked beetroot - diced
1tbsp balsamic vinegar
2tbsp brown sugar

1 red onion - chopped
50ml port wine
150ml red wine
150ml chicken stock
2tsp arrowroot
salt & pepper to taste

Trim the duck breasts and score the fat across the breasts keeping the cuts as close as possible to one another.
Season and refrigerate until ready for use.
When ready place the duck in a non-stick pan - fat side down.
Cook until dark and then turn over cooking for a further 20 seconds.
Remove and place in oven at approximately 370°F for 5 - 6 minutes.
Remove duck from pan and allow to rest for a few minutes. Drain some of the fat into the pigeon peas and stir well.

Pan fry the pancetta, add the pigeon peas, chopped parsley and 50ml of port wine and reduce to a syrup consistency.
Add 75ml chicken stock and reduce by two thirds.
Keep warm.

Warm the orange juice in a pan and reduce by one third.
Add the beetroot, balsamic vinegar and brown sugar.
Cook gently until reaching a syrup consistency.
Keep warm.

Sweat the red onion, add the port and red wine and reduce by one third.
Add the chicken stock and reduce again by one third.
Mix the arrowroot with a little water and add to the sauce. Cook to thicken and season to taste.
Keep warm.

# Assiette of Chocolate

Grenada is acknowledged as having some of the best chocolate in the world. Evidence of this can be found in the form of this organic hand made chocolate, from the Grenada Chocolate Factory, which is to be found in selected gourmet stores around London.

*"This dish is for chocolate lovers to die for… or at least do a little bit more work than usual as it combines three separate chocolate-based concoctions! It's appearance at the table is normally accompanied by sighs of … well shall we just say sighs and leave it at that?"*

### Soufflé Base
**Ingredients**
Serves 8

250ml milk
75g icing sugar
1 vanilla pod or 1tsp vanilla essence
2 egg yolks
20g cornstarch
125g good quality plain chocolate

### Soufflé Finish
**Ingredients**

4 egg whites
2 egg yolks
63g icing sugar

### White Chocolate Sorbet
**Ingredients**

240g good quality white chocolate
500ml water
170g caster sugar

Line 8 x 2oz ramekins with melted butter and white sugar.
Bring milk and vanilla pod/essence to the boil.
Beat icing sugar, egg yolks and cornstarch together.
Pour boiling milk on to the egg yolk mix, return to heat and thicken.
Stir in melted chocolate.
Pour mixture into a clean mixing bowl, cover with buttered greaseproof paper and cool until tepid.

Whisk the egg whites until peaked and gradually add the icing sugar until stiff.
Fold egg yolks into the soufflé base mix and add ⅓ of the meringue mix to loosen.
Fold in the remaining meringue mix and divide between the ramekins.
Bake in a water bath in a hot oven (400°F) until raised.
This should take approx. 10 - 15 minutes.

Bring the water and sugar to the boil.
Remove pan from heat, add chocolate and stir until melted.
Pass mixture through a sieve and chill.
When chilled, put in an ice-cream maker and churn until as thick as possible.

## Ricotta and White Chocolate Mousse
### Ingredients

90g ricotta cheese
90g sour cream
160ml double cream
1`tbsp gelatine
40ml cold water
70g caster sugar
4 egg whites
60g good quality white chocolate

Line 8 small plastic molds - 1½ inches in diameter – with acetate strips.
Semi whip cream until it forms soft peaks.
Fold cream into ricotta and sour cream.
Sprinkle gelatine into the 40ml of cold water and let stand for one minute.
Put the sugar in a mixing bowl, stir in the egg whites and place the bowl over a bain marie*, whisking the egg white mixture continuously until the temperature reaches 65°C (140°F). This is to make meringue mix.
Remove mixture from heat and continue whisking until cool.
Warm gelatine mix until dissolved and add to the melted white chocolate.
Add the chocolate to ⅓ of the meringue mix stirring quickly.
Add this mix to the remaining meringue mix.
Fold in the cream and cheese mixture.
Pour into prepared mould and place in fridge to set.

## Chocolate Sauce
### Ingredients

200g good quality plain chocolate
150ml milk
4tbsp double cream
30g caster sugar
30g butter

Melt the chocolate in a bain marie.
Bring milk, cream and sugar to the boil.
Pour onto the melted chocolate stirring all the time.
Take the pan off the heat and beat in the butter.

*"These 3 desserts are served as a platter. The sorbet is served in a biscuit cup, the soufflé is dusted with icing sugar before presentation and the mousse is set in a plastic cone mould. Chocolate sauce is then put on the plate. Final presentation depends on the imagination and flair of the chef!"*

*see glossary

# Cardamom baked
## custards

Cardamom is not indigenous to the Caribbean, but is heavily cultivated in countries such as India and Sri Lanka. It comes from the ginger plant and in many of these locations it is used more than cinnamon. However, the 'bite' in this recipe comes from the cashew nuts placed in the bottom of the dish. Cashew trees are a common sight here in Grenada, but cashews are not an export product.

*"The good news is that they are harvested, roasted and bottled locally. You will find them delicious and readily available in many of the small locally owned spice shops for which the island is renowned."*

### Cardamom Baked Custards
#### Ingredients
Serves 8

250ml unsweetened coconut milk
1tsp ground cardamom
¼ tsp finely ground mixed spice
1tsp ground nutmeg
50g golden syrup
3 eggs
¼ tsp vanilla essence
40g brown sugar
1tbsp cooking oil
25 cashew nuts - whole

Bring milk, spices and golden syrup to the boil. Leave to infuse for 10 minutes.
Beat the eggs, vanilla essence and brown sugar and gently whisk the milk mixture into them.
Grease ramekins or use flexi-pan muffin moulds.
Lay several cashew nuts in each mould and pour egg mixture over them.
Bake in a bain-marie for 40 minutes or until set.
Serve with wedges of fresh mango or papaya and cinnamon whipped cream.

### Cinnamon Whipped Cream
#### Ingredients

118ml (¼ pint) of cream
113g icing sugar
½ tsp cinnamon

Whip cream to a soft peak.
Add icing sugar and cinnamon and refrigerate before use.

#  anana and coconut cream

## in a caramel glass box

It was once a common sight on visiting the island, to see rows and rows of what appeared to be blue plastic bags attached to banana trees all along the roadsides as you traversed the island. These bags actually covered the 'hands' of bananas that would be picked and used for export purposes. With the demise of the export market this is no longer a common sight.

For domestic consumption though, bananas or 'figs' are plentiful in all manner of varieties, textures and sweetness.

*"If you are on the Isle of Spice why not try some of those which you do not often see on supermarket shelves. The small fat 'finger' ones are succulent and great favourites."*

### Banana & Coconut Cream
**Ingredients**
Serves 10

250ml water
250g sugar
1 cinnamon stick

1 lime - juice only
400ml double cream
4 bananas – chopped and liquidized
100ml coconut cream
2pkts gelatine - 7g each

### Caramel Glass Paste
**Ingredients**

620g butter
620g icing sugar
120ml corn syrup
340g flour

Make a syrup - boil water sugar and cinnamon stick and simmer for 10 minutes.
Peel bananas and poach in syrup until tender.
Blend the bananas whilst they are still warm, add lime juice to stop them from going black. Add the coconut cream.
Warm the bloomed gelatine and add to this mixture.
Whip the cream until it reaches ribbon stage, fold into banana mix.
Chill the mixture for approximatley 3 - 4 hours
When set, pipe mix into caramel box and serve immediately.

Cream butter and sugar until soft. Add corn syrup and mix to combine. Stir in flour.
Cut rectangle shaped stencil - a plastic ice cream container lid can be used. Place stencil on greaseproof paper and smooth paste thinly over cut shape.
Remove stencil.
Bake caramel paste on 350°F for 4 - 6 minutes.
Remove baked caramel and mould around a cylindrical instrument such as rolling pin.
When moulded caramel is set, pipe set banana cream mix into 'box' and serve.

# Farine pudding

Farine comes from the root crop - cassava, which may also be known as manioc or yuca depending which of the islands you come from. Preparing farine from scratch may seem like hard work. This is done by boiling the root in water for at least 45 minutes and then discarding the water. Alternatively, you can grate the cassava and place it in a muslin cloth and then squeeze out as much of the acid as possible before cooking.

*"For those of us who are living life at too fast a pace for all that work, ready-to-use farine is available in supermarkets and grocery stores. If you take the easy route, you'll have more than enough energy to try this simple but tasty recipe."*

### Farine Pudding
**Ingredients**
Serves 8 - 10

12tbsp farine
1½ cups of sugar
2tsp vanilla essence
2tsp lime rind - finely grated
4 tins evaporated milk (414 ml each)
3tbsp gelatine
3tbsp rum
1 litre whipping cream - whipped to soft peak
120ml (¼ pint) pate a bombe*
(see pg 64 for method)

### Pate a Bombe
**Ingredients**

6 egg yolks
800ml stock syrup

**B**ring evaporated milk, sugar, lime and vanilla essence to the boil, until the sugar dissolves.
Add the farine to the milk and sugar mix and cook for a further 5 minutes, stirring to ensure that the farine does not burn at the bottom.

**S**prinkle the gelatine onto the rum and leave to stand for 10 minutes until the gelatine has bloomed.
Warm the gelatine mix until it is liquid and add to the warm farine mix.
Place the mixture over a bowl of ice and leave to cool, stirring occassionally.

**W**hen the farine is beginning to set, mix in the pate a bombe and them fold in whipping cream.
Pour mixture into medium sized, lightly greased pirex dish and place in fridge for minimum of 3 hours.
*Cut into portions as required..*

**W**hisk egg yolks and syrup in a bowl over a bain marie for approx. 20 minutes, until mix thickens reaching 65°C.
Allow mixture to cool and fold in whipped cream.
This is a base for parfait.

*\*see glossary*

# Nutmeg and guava stew
## in a sweet almond crepe

You cannot speak about Grenada without mentioning spices and most particularly nutmeg. But to understand the true versatility of nutmeg you have to ask a Grenadian. No part of the nutmeg is wasted here. You will taste its rich flavour in a wide variety of Grenadian cuisine from meats to jams and syrups and even liqueur. Nutmeg is also reputed to have certain magical powers which will be of interest to some, but we'll stick with what we know, and we know you will enjoy the recipe below.

*"Oh nearly forgot to say that a rum punch here without nutmeg grated on it is definitely not a Grenadian beverage!"*

### Nutmeg and Guava Stew
**Ingredients**
Serves 8

200g nutmeg stew
200g guava stew
1 cinnamon stick
1 vanilla pod - split & de-seeded

Place all ingredients in a thick bottomed pan.
Bring to boil and then simmer for approx 10 - 15 mins or until fruit falls apart.

### Sweet Almond Crêpe
**Ingredients**

250g flour
2 whole eggs
2 egg yolks
475ml milk
½ tsp almond essence
2 limes - grated zest only
100g butter – for buerre noisette*

Beat flour, milk, eggs, cream, vanilla and almond essence and lemon zest together. Strain to remove any lumps. Stir in buerre noisette.*
Leave to stand for 15 minutes before use.
Heat a knob of butter in a medium size non stick frying pan and pour in ⅓ cup of crêpe batter. Spread well. Cook over medium heat and ensure that the crêpe is well cooked on both sides.

Arrange the crêpes and stew as per your preference, using a little imagination.

*see glossary*

62

# cocoa tea parfait

## Mark Banthorpe - Signature Dish

### Chocolate Tea Cups
**Ingredients**
Serves 10

453g (1lb) melted dark chocolate
roll of clingfilm

Brush the inside of a flexi silicone muffin tray with melted chocolate and refrigerate for 20 minutes.
Repeat this procedure a minimum of twice more, refrigerating each time.
On final brushing with chocolate, leave to refrigerate for at least 40 minutes.
Remove from muffin tray when ready for use.

### Cocoa Tea Base
**Ingredients**

1 ball cocoa - 57g
250ml water
75g white sugar
2tbsp cream
1 packet of gelatine – 7g
25ml dark rum

Boil water and cocoa ball until the cocoa ball dissolves.
Pass through a fine strainer to remove any lumps.
Add the sugar and cream and leave until sugar is dissolved.
Dissolve the gelatine in the rum for 10 - 15 minutes to soften.
Warm liquid in the microwave to dissolve and add to the still warm cocoa mix.
Put aside.

### Pate a Bombe
**Ingredients**

6 egg yolks
250g white sugar

Place the sugar into a heavy bottom saucepan and add water until it resembles wet sand.
Put on a high heat and using a candy/sugar thermometer bring to a temperature of 116°C.
Whilst the sugar is reaching the correct temperature, place egg yolks in a mixing machine bowl and put on a whisk attachment.
When the sugar reaches 116°C, turn the mixer onto medium speed and gradually pour the sugar onto the yolks.
Continue to mix until the mixture becomes cool.

## Tuille Mix
### Ingredients

175g flour
175g sugar
100g butter - melted
100g egg whites

## For Presentation
### Ingredients

250ml whipping cream
142g white marzipan
icing sugar for decoration
100ml whipping cream
1tsp cinnamon

## Assembling the Dessert

Beat egg whites with sugar until frothy.
Melt butter, add to egg white mix, then add flour and mix until it reaches a smooth paste consistency.
Put the tuille mix into a piping bag with a 3 - 4mm piping nozzle.
Pipe wavy lines on greaseproof paper to resemble steam and bake until golden brown.
You will need 3 - 4 pieces per dessert.

Whip 250ml whipping cream to soft peaks.
Cut marzipan into ½ inch pieces and dip into sugar syrup and then granulated sugar to resemble sugar cubes.
Whip the 100ml whipping cream to soft peaks for decorating the desserts.

Place cocoa tea base mix in a large bowl and add the pate a bombe mix until homogenous.
Fold in the 250ml of semi whipped cream. Divide this mix between the chocolate cups and place in the fridge to set.

Place a teaspoon onto a large plate and dust with cocoa powder so as to leave the imprint of the spoon.
Place the marzipan 'sugar' cubes next to the spoon.
Place a set cocoa cup onto each plate.
Pipe a little cream on top of the 'cup' filled with base mix and sprinkle a little cinnamon on top of each.
Place three tuilles in each cup and serve.

# Glossary

| Term | Explanation |
| --- | --- |
| Bain-marie | The bain-marie consists of a large container (i.e. a pirex dish) filled with a working liquid (usually water) and another, smaller container filled with the substance to be heated. The smaller container is partially immersed in the larger container, and the larger container is heated. |
| Buerre Noisette | French term for "brown butter" or literally "hazelnut butter". Butter is cooked in a pan until it turns a golden brown. The resulting butter has a nutty flavor. |
| Callaloo | Callaloo, some say is like spinach. It's a favourite in the Caribbean diet. As versatile a vegetable as you could ever wish to eat, it is the leaf of the root vegetable, dasheen. |
| Chervil | Also known as French parsley this is one of the components of the four fine herbes. It has a delicate liquorice flavor with the mild pepperiness of parsley. It is a fleeting flavor. Cooking and drying destroys the subtle flavor, so use large quantities of fresh leaves, toward the end of cooking. |
| Chives/Scallions | Both of these are alternative names for spring onions. |
| Farce | Minced or finely chopped, usually as a stuffing. |

| | |
|---|---|
| **Fish Fumet** | A highly concentrated fish stock used for poaching fish or for fish sauces. It is made by reducing well-flavoured fish stock. Fish fumet is a concentrated version of fish stock. It is made with vegetables (leeks, onion, and celery), spices, water, wine, and fish bones (fish heads can be used, but you should remove the eyes). To make it, you "sweat" the vegetables in a pan, then add the fish bones and spices. When the bones start to break down, you add wine and reduce. Then, add the water and proceed as for fish stock (cook for 30-45 minutes). |
| **Mire poix** | Mixed vegetables. Mirepoix is a mixture of diced onions, carrots, celery and leeks. |
| **Pate a bombe** | This term is used for egg yolks beaten with a sugar syrup, then aerated. It is the base used for many mousse and buttercream recipes. |
| **Ramekin** | Individual portion size baking dish |
| **Roux** | A mixture of flour and fat that is cooked over a low heat and used to thicken soups and sauces. There are three types of roux: white, blond, and brown. White and Blond Roux are both made with butter and used in cream sauces while Brown Roux can be made with either butter or the drippings from what you are cooking. It is used for darker soups and sauces. |
| **Shado – Beni** | This is more commonly found in the Caribbean but can be interchanged with coriander or cilantro for any recipe, as they all hail from the same family. |
| **Seasoning Peppers** | Small pungent peppers which are very common in the Caribbean, They are not hot and you can substitute with bell peppers if they are not available. |
| **Tomato Concasse** | Tomatoes, peeled, chopped and de-seeded. |

# Notes

1 ounce is the same as 28.34 grammes

1 pint is the same as .473ml

1 kg is the same as 2.2llbs

116 centigrade is equal to 240.8 farenheit